CW01395498

EXPANDING World of DATA

Tom Jackson

OXFORD
UNIVERSITY PRESS

OXFORD
UNIVERSITY PRESS

Great Clarendon Street, Oxford OX2 6DP

Oxford is a registered trade mark of
Oxford University Press in the UK and in certain other countries

© Oxford University Press 2023
Text written by Tom Jackson
Illustrated by Ekaterina Gorelova and Ana Seixas

Designed and edited by Raspberry Books Ltd

First published 2023

British Library Cataloguing in Publication Data:

ISBN 978-0-19-278316-5

1 3 5 7 9 10 8 6 4 2

Printed in China

Paper used in the production of this book is a natural,
recyclable product made from wood grown in sustainable forests.
The manufacturing process conforms to the environmental regulations
of the country of origin.

Acknowledgements

The publisher and authors would like to
thank the following for permission to use
photographs and other copyright material:

Cover artwork: Ekaterina Gorelova and
Ana Seixas; photos: Pavlo S/Shutterstock;
Aleksandr Bryliaev/Shutterstock and author.
Inside artwork: Photos: 1(tl): Pavlo S/
Shutterstock; p5: DW labs Incorporated/
Shutterstock; p12: Eric Isselee/Shutterstock;
p18: Johan Larson/Shutterstock; p19:
DenysHolovtiuk/Shutterstock;

p24: Jim Cumming/Shutterstock; p47:
Morphart creation; pp60-61: muratart/
Shutterstock.

Artwork by **Ekaterina Gorelova**, **Ana Seixas**,
Aaron Cushley, and Raspberry Books.

Every effort has been made to contact
copyright holders of material reproduced
in this book. Any omissions will be rectified
in subsequent printings if notice is given to
the publisher.

Did you know that we also publish Oxford's bestselling
and award-winning **Very Short Introductions** series?
These are perfect for adults and students
www.veryshortintroductions.com

Contents

Chapter 1

Collecting Data

Data is a little word with a big meaning. Put very simply, data is information which is most often collected as numbers. Data allows us to answer the questions we have about the world. We take records and make measurements and use them to tell us what is true and what is not.

Data is being collected about all of us, including you, every day. It can tell us where people live, where they go, what they buy—even who their friends are. This personal data can reveal things **about you** that perhaps even you did not know! Even **qualitative** data like this is converted to numbers at some point.

This book shows you how using data gives us **superpowers** to learn new things, unlock hidden mysteries, and even predict the future.

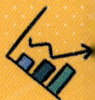

❋ Speak like a scientist ❋

DATUM

The word 'data' properly refers to many bits of information. One piece of information is known as a datum. The number of sweets you may have in your pocket now is a datum, but the record of how many sweets you eat every day of the week is data.

datum

Data helped create the first civilizations many thousands of years ago as people recorded what they owned and where they lived. This helped them organize society and learn to live together in bigger communities. Ever since then, data has been used to help us understand where we fit in the world.

In the sixteenth century, Polish scientist Nicolas Copernicus studied how the stars and planets moved through the sky.

Using the data he collected, Copernicus was able to show that Earth was not at the centre of the Universe as people believed, but instead was moving around the Sun and was one of several other planets. That's an **enormous** shift in the way people thought about the world and it was all done using data.

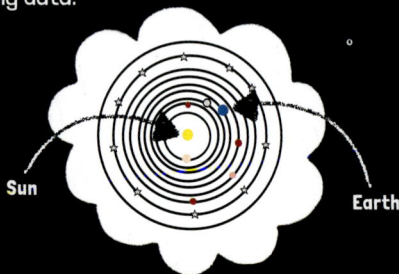

Sun

Earth

Data is at the heart of discovery. Scientists have shown that the only way to really find out how something works—that could be a star, a tsunami, or a sneeze—is to collect data about it. That data will contain the answers to whatever mysteries you want to solve.

Data is also used in many ways that affect us directly. Doctors use data to track the spread of diseases and to test how well new treatments work. **Engineers** use it to test their designs, scientists learn from it, and teachers use data to measure your progress at school. The final score of a sports match is a piece of data which is especially important for the fans!

Data is everywhere—so let's learn more about it. Read on and discover:

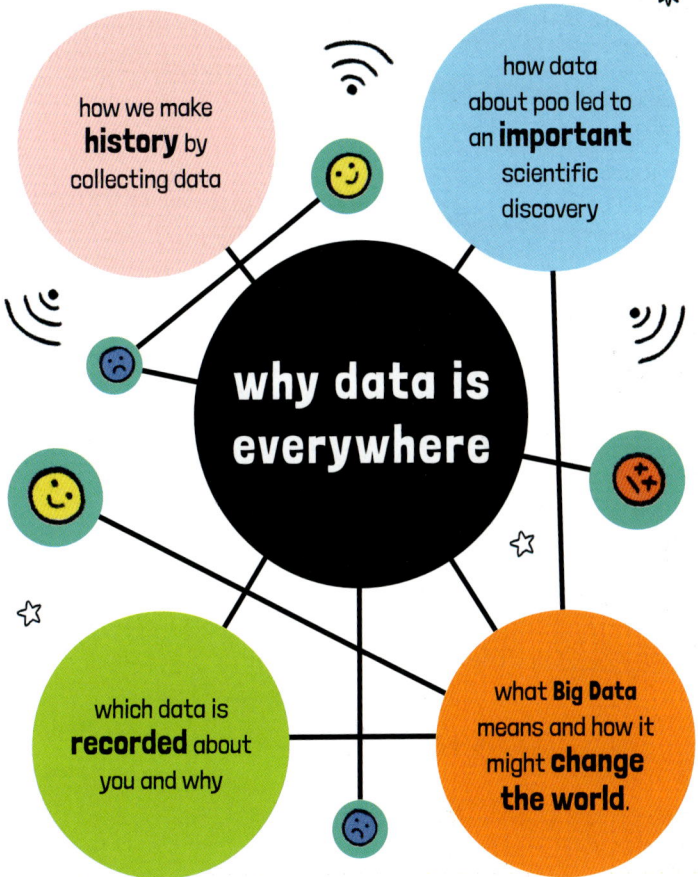

how we make **history** by collecting data

how data about poo led to an **important** scientific discovery

why data is everywhere

which data is **recorded** about you and why

what **Big Data** means and how it might **change the world**.

Let's begin our deep dive into the **expanding world of data.**

Chapter 2

Learning to Count

Data is a way of discovering patterns and meaning which can help us understand how things work.

There are lots of ways that we can capture information about the world around us. We can paint a picture of a thunderstorm or write a story about a chemical explosion, but not everyone will understand what these descriptions are saying exactly. Data can tell us *exactly* how many lightning flashes there were last night and how hot the explosion got. Data can then be checked and rechecked to make sure it's accurate.

When we collect data, we can see certain patterns emerge which can be a very powerful tool for finding stuff out. The numbers within the data might even contain **hidden information** that we didn't mean to record. We can unlock the secrets of data if we know how to ask the right questions.

Comparing sets of data that were made in different places or at different times is a great way to do this. The ways that data is the same or different can tell us something interesting about the world. For example, comparing the rainfall and temperature records for Manchester in England, and Málaga in Spain, will tell you which place is best for a warm and dry summer holiday!

I should have gone to Spain.

Comparing sets of data only works if they are recorded in the same way, using the same system for every kind of information. That system took some time to get organized. Let's venture into the distant past to **find out more about it.**

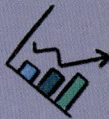

Making history

The first time anyone said the word 'data' was about 400 years ago. However, people had been using the idea of data for thousands of years—it's probably the first thing to be recorded in history. We use the term '**recorded history**' to mean the period of the past when people were making records of what was going on at the time. That includes counting what they had—and that's data. Before this, writing and recording data didn't exist and so this earlier period is called **prehistoric**.

Balls of clay

The very first clear historical records were made around 7,000 years ago in a place called Sumer. This was one of the world's first civilizations, in what is now Iraq. These ancient Sumerian records were data— although perhaps not quite as we know it.

tokens

The data being recorded in Sumer was information about numbers of sheep and cows, and how many bags of wheat or fleeces of wool had been produced that year. Each item was represented by a clay token with a certain shape. Farmers gathered the correct number of different tokens which were then sealed inside a hollow clay ball called a *bulla*.

Tax collectors would break the bulla open, using the tokens inside to calculate how much of the farmer's wealth needed to be paid to the king or queen. The tokens inside the bulla represented what it was worth.

Today, archaeologists use data from ancient bullas to learn more about Sumer. The data gives us a detailed picture of who was living there, whether they were poor or wealthy, and how their communities changed over time.

a bulla

Simpler symbols

The token system probably grew out of a simpler idea: shepherds would make a pile of pebbles, one for every sheep, enabling them to check that the number of sheep was still the same as the number of pebbles at the end of the day. For centuries, small stones were used as counters. The Roman word for stone is *calx*, and little stones are calculi. Maths puzzles are known today as calculations because of this.

Today, we use **numerals** rather than tokens to represent data.

Numerals are a brilliant invention because they can record any number or value which can be written on paper, displayed on a screen, drawn on a beach, scratched on a rock, wherever. The simplicity of our number system opens a world of possibility because it makes it easier to understand data of all kinds and to learn from it. We can then use numbers to share what we've discovered.

✳ Speak like a scientist ✳

NUMERALS

Numerals are the shaped symbols that represent particular numbers: 1 is one, 2 is two . . . I'm sure you know the rest. The Mayans of ancient Central America created their numerals using symbols for shells, stones, and sticks.

In Mayan numerals, a dot (a stone) means 1, while a bar (a stick) means 5.

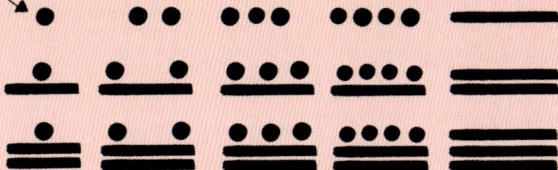

Making marks

One of the earliest examples of numerals are on the Ishango Bone, which was created in Central Africa about 20,000 years ago. The bone had marks **scratched** on it which looked like numbers. Similar marks, or **tallies**, have also been found scratched or drawn on rocks and wood.

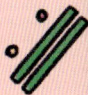

These marks were counting something, but we don't know what. Tallies like this were probably the first written numerals, and perhaps the first writing of any kind. Even today, tallies can be a good way to keep track of an amount, like the number of days spent on a desert island!

One mark represents the number one, two marks represents two, and so on. To make it easier to read **big** numbers, five and ten were replaced with different symbols. Ancient people all over the world built combinations of symbols that added up to the right value, in this way.

The Babylonians, a civilization living near to Sumer, used a symbol to represent one, creating clusters of this mark together in various ways to make bigger and bigger numbers. They wrote numbers as marks in wet clay using a reed, in a system called cuneiform. Once left to dry in the sun, the cuneiform clay tablets became a permanent data record that lasted for thousands of years—you can read them today in museums.

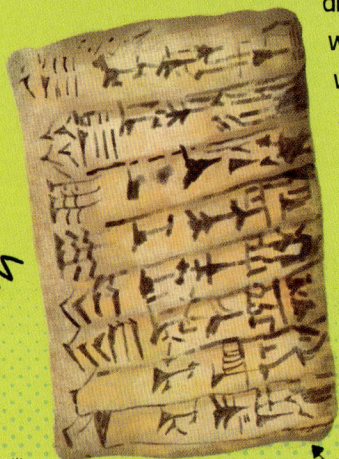

a cuneiform tablet

Babylonian numbers are hard to read, especially when large values are involved, and 2,000 years later the ancient Romans faced a similar challenge. You might be familiar with Roman numerals already—I is 1, V is 5, X is 10, C is 100—but larger numbers written in Roman numerals were **very long** indeed and hard to understand. To do sums, the ancient Romans moved stones on a board or in a tray of sand, in the same way an **abacus** works.

I can do that sum quicker with my top-of-the-range abacus!

* Speak like a scientist *

ABACUS

An abacus is a simple device, made from counters on rods, that can be used as a very effective calculator.

Adding zero

Roman numerals were used in Europe until as late as 500 years ago. By then, a new number system from Asia was becoming more popular because it made calculations a whole lot easier. The new system was known as Hindu-Arabic numerals . . . but you already know all about them and probably just call them 'numbers'.

Hindu-Arabic numbers, invented in India, were in use by the eighth century. The big difference from Roman numerals was that they used a number for nothing, known as zero. The system is constructed from sets of units, tens, hundreds, and so on. So the number 111 means one unit, one ten and one hundred.

The zero is an essential component, bridging the gap when a position in the number is not being counted. For example, in 101 the zero between the ones makes it clear we're showing one unit and one hundred. Without the 0 the number reads as 11, which is **quite confusing!**

This system, called **positional numbers**, was being used across South Asia for centuries, while much of the rest of the world wrestled with more clunky systems.

Fibonacci, a young Italian mathematician travelling in North Africa in the twelfth century, came across the system while doing business with Arab traders. He helped introduce it into Europe, although it took centuries for positional numbers to take over from Roman numerals.

And that's how zero works!

Fibonacci

That's clever!

17

−5 −4 −3 −2 −1 0 +1 +2 +3 +4 +5

From the fourteenth century, people began to use symbols for maths operations—things like +, −, =, the signs for plus, minus, and equals. Before that, calculations were written out as sentences using words. Now mathematicians, traders, and farmers were able to calculate faster and with fewer mistakes.

Less than nothing

As well as making numbers clearer and more precise, the inventor of zero, the Indian mathematician Brahmagupta, had an even bigger idea: he used zero as a number just like any other. This made it possible to record zero (for example, one year a farmer produces zero bags of wheat). That might not seem like a very important piece of data, but it makes it possible to **compare** how the number of bags of wheat varies, year to year.

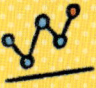

Brahmagupta put zero before one on the number line. One was no longer the first number: adding 1 to 0 made 1. Subtracting 1 from 1 made 0. So what happens if you subtract 1 from 0? The answer is −1. The number line no longer started with zero. Zero is in the middle, with **positive** numbers going one way and **negative** ones going the other.

Now the farmer compares last year's records with this year's and calculates that the difference in the number of bags of wheat from last year is −5. The record also shows the number of sheep went up by +10. Maybe the sheep ate all the wheat?! Does this matter if the sheep are more profitable than the wheat? Data can help with that question too.

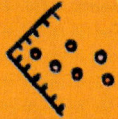

DATA HERO

BRAHMAGUPTA

Indian mathematician who invented the idea of zero in the seventh century.

Measure up

A system of measurements is where the length and weight of objects are recorded as a number of units. As long as everyone uses the same units, then everyone can agree that the measurements are **accurate** and can be **trusted**.

To compare the values of sheep and wheat, the farmer will need a system of measurements. At the market, customers want to know that each bag contains the same amount of wheat. Farmers also need to know how big their fields are so they can figure out how much space to devote to animals or crops.

In Sumer, length was measured in cubits—the length of the forearm from elbow to fingertip. But people's arms are all different lengths, and so cubits might be different lengths too. Let's say a bag of wheat was a cubit wide and a cubit tall. What happens if one farmer had long arms and huge hands and another had very short fingers? A cubit measured by each would be different, and the long-fingered farmer's bags would hold more wheat but still cost the same as a neighbour's.

For centuries, the way to overcome this lack of accuracy was for a king, queen, emperor, or other ruler to set a standard for each unit. A measuring rod was made to an exact length and copies were sent around the country for government officials to use. But it was easy to cheat or make mistakes.

Ordinary people lost trust in the system, thinking they were being **swindled** whenever they bought food by weight or land by area. In France, this mistrust was one of the reasons for the start of the French Revolution. In the 1790s, after the French Revolution, the new government asked mathematicians and scientists to think up a new system of measurements. The result was today's metric system. All the units were based on 'natural constants'—things we can measure in nature that never change.

The process started with choosing a unit of length, defined as one metre. Europe's best land surveyors estimated that the distance from the Earth's Equator to the North Pole was equal to ten million metres. So one metre (m) = a ten-millionth of the distance from the Equator to the North Pole. The calculation wasn't terribly accurate, but it did give us a specific unit of length which all other units were based on.

area: hectare (ha) = area of square with sides 100 m long

volume: litre (l) = capacity of a cube with sides of 10 cm

weight: kilogram (kg) = weight of a litre of water

We want equality!

And a metric system!

10011101011

International system

Today, more advanced methods have been used to set the standard units of measurements for things like time, electric current, brightness of light, and temperature. Together they make up the **International System of Units.** They can be combined to measure anything you can think of. These standard units are agreed all over the world. Over time, people found that the data they collected became a treasure trove of facts.

11011000

Chapter 3

Finding Answers

Data is a way of finding out what might or might not be true. There are a lot of things that we think are true, but the data proves otherwise.

Which of these statements is **true?**

Wolves only howl when there is a full moon.

Mice love eating cheese.

Lightning never strikes in the same place twice.

You might have heard these statements presented as facts before, but people have collected data to investigate and discovered that none of these so-called facts are true! A wolf will howl just as much on a dark night as when there is a full moon. Given the choice, mice prefer to eat sweet food, and there are eight million lightning strikes hitting the ground every day, often striking in the same place. For example, the Empire State Building in New York City gets hit by lightning around 100 times a year!

Scientific methods

The best way to find out if something is **true or false** is to use the Scientific Method—a system used by scientists in their investigations. It has four steps:

- Observe the world and look for a mystery to investigate.

- Come up with an explanation for that mystery. This explanation is called the **hypothesis.**

- Carry out an experiment that tests the hypothesis. The measurements you collect during the experiment are your data.

- Analyze, or examine, the data to find out the result. Was your hypothesis true or false?

The great thing about the Scientific Method is that there's no such thing as a **wrong answer**. Even if the hypothesis was proven false, you've still learned something from the data. And then you can think of a new hypothesis.

Heavy meals

In the early seventeenth century, Santorio, an Italian doctor, was one of the first people to use data in a scientific investigation, asking himself, **'What happens to my food after I've eaten it?'** Santorio didn't have a hypothesis exactly, but he wanted to collect data to try and solve this mystery. He started weighing everything he ate and drank, keeping a careful record of how much he weighed before and after each meal, and he also weighed his **poo** and **wee**. He did this every day for **thirty years!**

Santorio's data-gathering was the first step in **understanding digestion and metabolism.**

What is typical?

The data Santorio collected was quite messy . . . and not just because of what he was measuring! The term 'messy' here means that the measurements are highly

varied and seem to change a lot from one day to the next. This can make it harder to figure out what the data is telling us. A simple way to analyze variable data is to use **averages**.

An average is a kind of middle figure that tells us something about a set of data in a quick and simple way. There are actually three kinds of average: the **mean**, the **mode**, and the **median**. They are all a little different to one another and have different uses.

Most football fans would not use averages to choose which team to support, but maybe they should! Let's look at the

scores of two rival football teams after playing twenty matches. What do the average scores tell us about which team is better?

Goalsville Rovers	0	0	1	1	1	1	1	1	1	1	1	1	1	1	1	1	2	2	2	2
Soccertown United	0	0	0	0	0	0	0	0	0	1	1	1	2	2	2	2	3	4	6	

Getting the mean

A good team scores a lot of goals. Soccertown United score twenty-four goals and Goalsville Rovers score twenty-two. Does that mean that Soccertown is the **best team?** To investigate further, we could find the mean score of each team.

You calculate the mean score by adding up all the goals and dividing this by the number of matches. Soccertown's mean score is:

$$24 \div 20 = 1.2$$

Goalsville do less well as their mean score is:

$$22 \div 20 = 1.1$$

The mean suggests that Soccertown is the better team.

✹ Speak like a scientist ✹

PRECISION

Precision means how exact a number is. The number 1.2 is more accurate than 1 but less accurate than 1.23. Numbers can be rounded up or down, to less accurate figures, to make them easier to use in calculations.

The mode

Although the mean scores are precise, they may not be the best average to use for judging which team to support. Soccertown United actually scored nothing in the first ten games, only one goal per game in the next three, and the other twenty-one goals were all scored in the last seven games. Meanwhile, Goalsville Rovers scored once in most of their matches, sometimes two goals, and sometimes none. The mean scores do not tell us about this aspect of the data, but another average, the mode, does. The mode is simply the most common value in the data.

So for the Soccertown scores, the mode is zero. Meanwhile, Goalsville's mode is one. This tells us that in most of the matches, Goalsville scored a higher number of goals than Soccertown. So which is the best team now? Maybe the third average, the median, will help to settle that question.

A better answer

The median takes some sorting out. It's the number dividing the upper half of the data from the lower half. It's found by **arranging** the data in order and finding the number that's in the middle. There's an even number of data here so there's no single middle number. We can just take the two middle numbers and find the halfway point between them. The Goalsville data is mostly 1s and that's also the median score. Soccertown's median score is between 0 and 1, so is 0.5.

We've **analyzed** the goals data on page 29 a bit more now and found this:

	Goalsville Rovers	Soccertown United
mean number of goals	1.1	1.2
mode number of goals	1	0
median score	1	0.5
range	2	6

The mode and median figures show that Goalsville scored goals in more games than Soccerville did and so won or drew more often. However, the mean also shows that when the team lost to Soccertown, they lost badly. The data says that Goalsville are the better team.

Being accurate

Football is a low-scoring game, and some matches have no goals at all, so sets of scoring data have a low range. For example, it's only two in the case of Goalsville. Because the **range** of the data is so small, a single goal added to the data can have a big difference on all three averages. It's therefore important that football scoring data is as **accurate** and **precise** as possible.

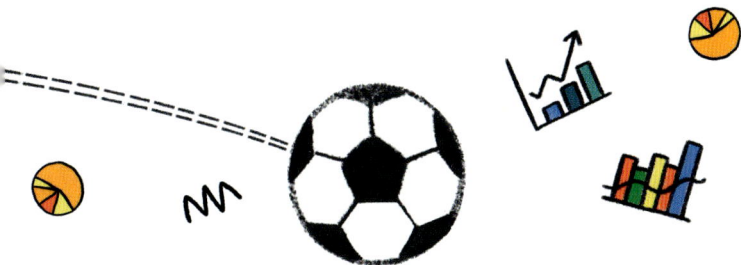

Speak like a scientist

RANGE

The range is the difference between the highest value in the data and the lowest.

However, accuracy and **precision** are less important for data with a wider spread of values and a much larger range between the lowest and highest values. It is impossible to measure some things, like a weight or a height, with 100 per cent accuracy because it is always possible that your measuring device, like a weighing scale or a ruler, may make an error. The important thing is for that error to be small enough not to change what the data tells us overall.

A guessing game

To win a football match, one team must score more goals than the other but not all competitions use exact numbers to decide a winner—some are guessing games. For example, people must guess how much a jar of sweets weighs: the winner is the person who guesses the closest to the actual weight.

There are a number of ways to make that guess, or estimate. You could pick up the jar to feel its weight, or you could weigh one sweet by itself, guess how many more there are in the jar, and then multiply the weight by that number (not forgetting to include an estimate of the weight of the jar itself of course).

It is very likely that no one will guess that exact weight but someone will be closer than the others, so they are the winner. Making estimates like this can be a very good way of measuring as long as you have enough people making guesses. This system is called the **'wisdom of the crowd'**.

Let's say 1,000 people enter the jar-of-sweets competition and no one guesses the exact weight to the nearest fraction of a gram. However, when we calculate the mean guess from all 1,000 guesses, that answer will be very close to the true figure. It turns out that many heads are better than one when it comes to making guesses! If we had no scales available, then this method would be the best one for measuring the jar's weight.

Personal experience

Scientists are also interested in collecting data about how people feel or experience things. For example, researchers might want to know how full people feel after eating certain foods or how frightened they feel when they watch a scary movie.

It is not possible to measure feelings with a ruler or set of scales. Instead, researchers often ask people to give a number, let's say between one and ten, which can help to give an estimate as to how they feel.

This kind of data is described as **psychometric** (sai-kho-**met**-ric) and there is no way to know how accurate a measure like this is because each person chooses their own score.

'Not scared at all.'

0 1 2 3 4 5

'Argghhh! Really, REALLY scared!'

✳ Speak like a scientist ✳

PSYCHOMETRIC DATA

Psychometric data measures how a person experiences and processes the world.

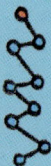

Researchers collecting a lot of data from a large number of people can learn some really interesting things. Perhaps the people who feel full after eating a bucket of popcorn are also the people who feel most frightened watching a scary movie? Is this true? Maybe someone could collect the data and find out.

Collection problems

Compared to counting goals or weighing jars of sweets, it's much easier to make mistakes using psychometric data. For example, when analyzing how people feel when they watch a scary movie, it's important that the data is collected from a wide group of people. An easy way to do this would be to go to a cinema showing the latest scary film and ask the audience how they felt when watching it.

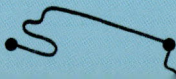

However, this data would only be from people who chose to see the film in the first place so might be **biased** towards people who already like scary films. Instead, it would be better to collect representative data, or data that represents everyone, not just data from the people who would pay to watch a scary film.

☀ Speak like a scientist ☀

BIASED

We say data is biased when it is badly collected or wrongly checked and so appears to show something is more important or common than it really is.

It can be challenging to find representative data, and one study is not enough. Data scientists know it is important to check how the data is collected. An extra final stage of the Scientific Method is to do the experiment and research again and again to test if the answer is the same each time.

Chapter 4

Seeing Data

Data scientists learned a long time ago that the best way to show what a data set (a group, or set of data) means is to turn it into a chart. There are many kinds of chart, but they all present data in a visual way that shows us things we cannot see from the numbers alone.

Mapping disease data

In 1854, an English doctor, John Snow, showed how **visual data** could be very useful when he made a chart mapping the spread of a stomach disease called cholera, in London. Cholera killed half the people who caught it. Most doctors believed the disease was spread by bad air, or miasma, which they said was an invisible substance that billowed out like a thick, slow-moving smoke from dead bodies. Cholera is actually caused by bacteria in poo that gets mixed into drinking water. In many parts of the world it is now rare.

When people in London became sick, the doctors caring for them assumed they were breathing in miasma. John Snow suspected otherwise, and so he began collecting data about **where** the cholera sufferers lived and **when** they became sick. Snow's data showed that all the sufferers had drunk water collected from the same pump on Broad Street, while their healthy neighbours got their water elsewhere.

Snow used his map to persuade the authorities to turn the pump off, and **the disease went away!**

Thanks to John Snow, when a serious disease starts to spread today, doctors rush to collect data that shows where the disease is coming from and how it is being spread.

Nursing data

Around the same time as Snow's data discovery, Florence Nightingale was the head nurse at a military hospital in Turkey, treating soldiers wounded in the Crimean War. Nightingale prioritized good hygiene practices on the wards which seems common sense to us today, but back then many doctors disagreed!

To prove her point, Nightingale created some charts, which she called rose diagrams. Today they are better known as pie charts.

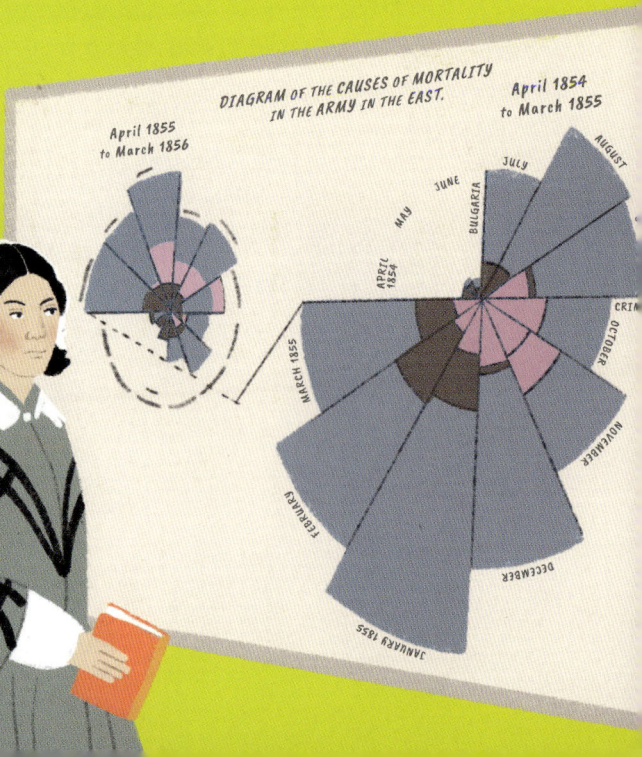

DIAGRAM OF THE CAUSES OF MORTALITY IN THE ARMY IN THE EAST.

April 1855 to March 1856

April 1854 to March 1855

AUGUST
JULY
JUNE
MAY
BULGARIA
APRIL 1854
MARCH 1855
CRIM
OCTOBER
NOVEMBER
DECEMBER
JANUARY 1855
FEBRUARY

Each section of the chart showed the number of soldiers dying every month in one year. The sections had coloured bands to show how many men died fighting and how many died from diseases, such as cholera. The first year of data from April 1854 showed that many more soldiers died from diseases rather than directly from war wounds. The chart also showed that once Nightingale's team of nurses worked in the hospital, deaths from diseases decreased.

Thanks to the **power** of her rose diagrams, Nightingale was able to show that her nursing system saved lives. As a result, she was asked to set up the world's first school of nursing in London.

DATA HERO

FLORENCE NIGHTINGALE

Used diagrams of her data to show that hospital patients were less likely to die if they were kept clean and comfortable by nurses.

Raising the bar

A Scottish economist called William Playfair was actually the first person to use charts to present data. In 1786, he wanted to find a way of comparing information about business in Britain, such as how much business was being done with different countries.

Playfair did this by inventing the bar chart. Each country had two bars, the length of one showing the imports and the length of the other showing the exports. It was easy to see which countries did the most business.

Drawing the line

Playfair also wanted to show how business changed from month to month and year to year, so instead of showing the data as a set of separate bars, he joined them all together as a line that **wiggled up and down.** Today, this is called a line graph. Playfair's line graph used the idea of horizontal and vertical **axes** invented by René Descartes (see page 46). A line which went up showed business increasing at that time. If the line went down, business was not doing so well. The line showed off these changes by filling in the gaps between each **data point**.

WILLIAM PLAYFAIR

Economist who invented ways
of displaying data such as the
bar chart and line graph.

EXPORTS AND IMPORTS FROM DENMARK AND NORWAY FROM 1700–1780

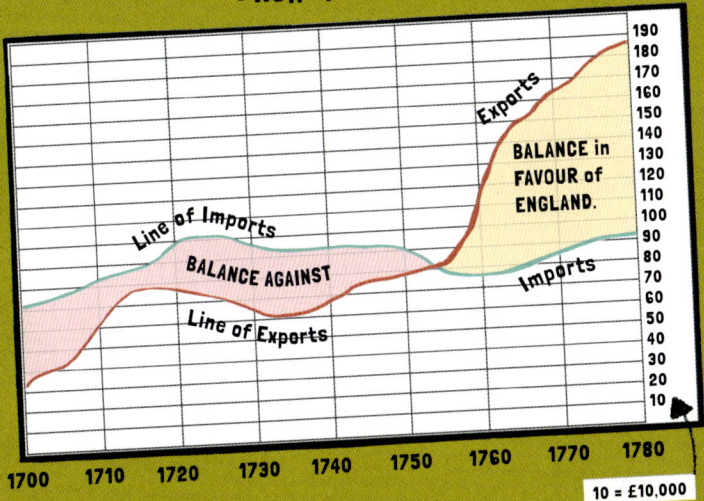

Exports

BALANCE in
FAVOUR of
ENGLAND.

Line of Imports

BALANCE AGAINST

Line of Exports

Imports

190 180 170 160 150 140 130 120 110 100 90 80 70 60 50 40 30 20 10

1700 1710 1720 1730 1740 1750 1760 1770 1780

10 = £10,000

Shaping up

Mathematicians might look at Playfair's line charts and
see that a line on a graph can be turned into an equation,
which might help us understand more about the data.

Descartes liked to spend a lot of time in bed, and one morning he watched a fly buzz around on the ceiling, weaving a curving path from place to place. Descartes thought that he could map the fly's journey by turning the ceiling into a grid of lines and connecting up all the places where the fly had landed. Each position was shown as two numbers, called **coordinates**. Every point on the grid had unique coordinates that were measured along two number lines, one horizontal, one vertical. These lines became known as axes. Point (1,1) is one unit along both axes, (2,1) is two horizontal moves and one vertical, and so on. You might know about coordinates already from games like Battleships.

Descartes realized that this system was not just a way of tracking routes, it could also be used to turn equations into lines.

Every coordinate is really a version of (x,y) where x is a number along the horizontal number line (the x axis) and y is a number along the vertical number line (the y axis). So the equation x = y creates the coordinates (1,1), (2,2), (3,3) and so on. The shape of the lines plotted on the graph would depend on the relationship between x and y in the equation.

DATA HERO

RENÉ DESCARTES

Invented coordinates which can be used to present data as a line chart. Descartes' system also allows us to turn lines into the mathematical equations that help us understand data better.

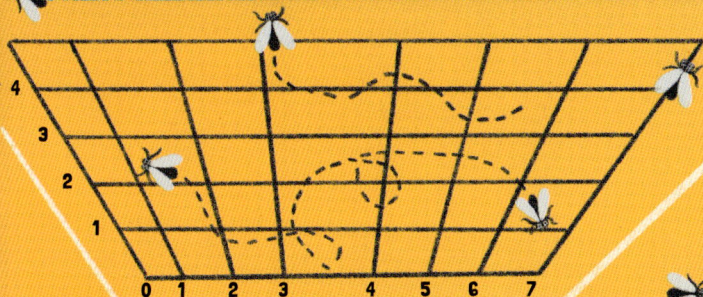

4
3
2
1

0 1 2 3 4 5 6 7

Bell curves

When data is plotted as a line, the shape of the line can reveal interesting features about it. If two sets of data seem to follow a similar line when plotted on the same graph, there must be similar links between the data in each set.

Imagine we collect the height of every adult living in a city—let's call it Mean City, we get a range of heights from very short to very tall people. Our measurements are not very precise, and everyone's height is rounded to the nearest centimetre, so many people are listed as having the same height.

If we plot a line based on the number of people who are the same height, we'll see a distinctive bell-shaped curve on our chart.

HEIGHT

Totally normal

The curve is highest in the middle because most
people in the city are not very tall nor very short, they
are somewhere in the middle, or of average height.
Data experts call the way measurements tend to be
arranged in a bell-shaped chart, a 'normal **distribution**'.
The bell-shaped normal distribution curve is exactly
symmetrical. Its three averages are all equal. The
mode, the most common value in the data, is shown
by the tallest part of the line, in the very middle.
The median is the halfway point in the data, and that
is in the very middle too. And the most typical value,
the mean, is found in exactly the same spot.

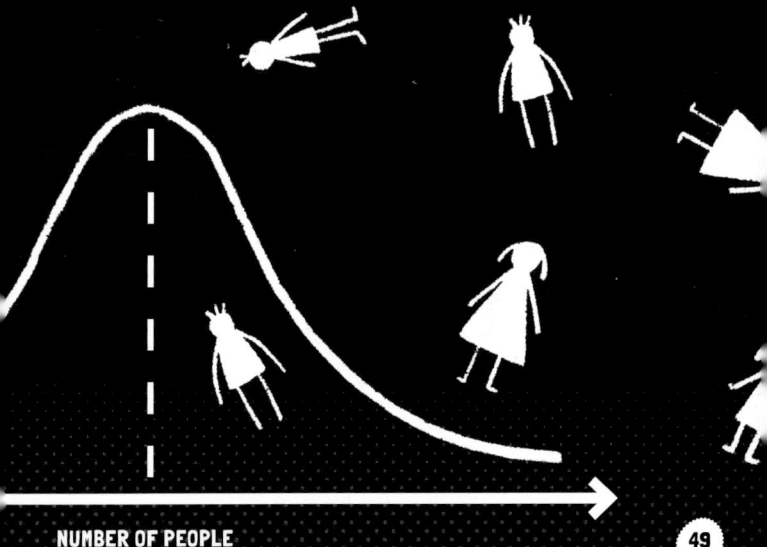

NUMBER OF PEOPLE

Skewed data

Measurement data doesn't always create a symmetrical bell-shaped curve. Sometimes the curve is skewed to one side, so the highest point on the curve isn't in the middle. A good example of this would be how much people in Mean City earn. In this case, the curve bulges to the left and flattens out to the right. The highest point on this skewed curve still shows us the mode. The median is still in the middle of the curve, but the mean is to the right. The change in shape is because most people earn below the mean amount. The mean is **distorted** away from the middle of the curve because a very small number of people will earn a huge amount of money.

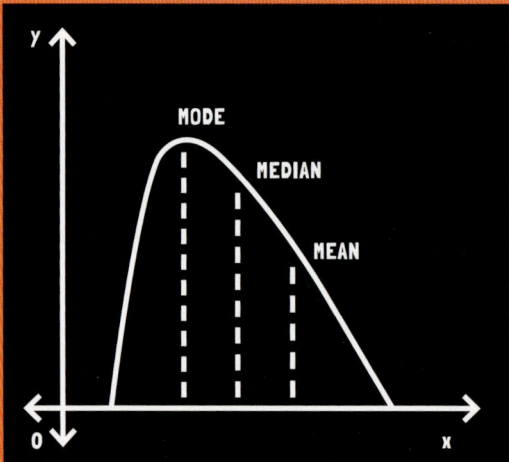

Is there a connection?

Data charts can be used to find links between different data sets. For example, we could do it with the height and earnings information using a scatter plot, where everyone in Mean City is shown as a point on the chart, creating dots **scattered** across the chart, in most cases, widely spaced out.

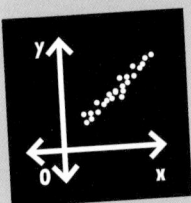

positive **correlation**

In the case of height and earnings, the dots cluster together to form an obvious shape, rising upwards from left to right. This clustering shows (regardless of gender), height and earnings are correlated (the two things have a relationship to one another, or are 'co-related'). The data seems to show that on average tall people earn more money than shorter people.

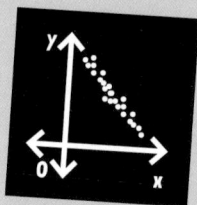

negative correlation

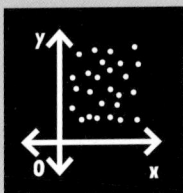

no correlation

Although height and earnings seem to be correlated, no one can really explain why and it may be there is no link at all. We would need to do more research to find out.

51

It is quite common for correlations to have no meaning at all . . .

The data shows that engineers also like eating mozerella.

Does this correlation tell us something?

OR IS IT MEANINGLESS?

lunch bag

I think I'll have fruit today instead.

The answer to these questions might seem obvious but how do we know for sure? Data experts have another good way of figuring out what is true: using the power of chance, which we will look at next.

Chapter 5

What are the Chances?

Experts in understanding data are called statisticians. They use data to create statistics, which are facts and figures that tell us something about the world.

However, just because data can be used to produce **statistics** **does not mean** that the statistics are always true. Data may be biased, or the results might just be coincidence, or a freak chance that makes the numbers appear to mean something when they do not.

✳ **Speak** like a **scientist** ✳

STATISTIC

A statistic is a result created from data which may tell us something true about the world. Statistics should not be believed until they have been carefully checked.

Chance is a number

Data experts use **probability** to check what the chances are that a statistic is true. Probability can tell us if a result is just a coincidence or if it is more than likely, or very likely, to be correct.

Probability is the mathematics of chance. The first people to become interested in it were gamblers playing games with dice, wanting to know when it was a good idea to bet money on a game and when it was better to give up. French mathematicians, Blaise Pascal and Pierre de Fermat, showed how to calculate the chances of winning and losing any game of chance.

✴ Speak like a scientist ✴

PROBABILITY

Probability is the scientific word for the effects of chance on the real world. Nothing is ever completely certain. Probablility calculates the chances of something happening or not.

For example, a dice has six sides and always lands with one side facing up. The **chance** of it landing on one side is the same as it is for any of the other five. If the aim of the game is to roll a six then you have a one-sixth chance of winning, and a five-sixths chance of rolling another number and losing. In other words, you're likely to lose the game five times for every time you win it.

DATA HEROES

BLAISE PASCAL AND PIERRE DE FERMAT

French mathematicians from the seventeenth century who worked together to create probability theory and the maths of chance, sharing their ideas in letters.

The big idea that Pascal and Fermat set out was that the chances of winning this game did not change the more you played it. The chances of winning or losing were the same with each roll. If you had lost five times already, you were not more likely to win on the sixth roll.

This is a common mistake a lot of people make. When you **toss a coin** you either get heads or tails. The chances of getting heads or tails is one in two.

Imagine tossing five heads in a row. Before you toss again, what do think the next result will be? We instinctively believe that because we've had a lot of heads already, we must be due to get tails next. This is just not true. The chances of getting tails is still the same as getting heads, just like it always was.

If you were to toss a coin many thousands of times and record the results, the data would show that you get almost half heads and half tails.

Under the curve

Probability and chance help us understand data. Let's go back to Mean City and, to keep it simple, let's say just 1,000 adults live there (it's a small place). The Mean City's height data could be presented as a bar chart made up from those 1,000 pieces of data. The tops of the bars create the same bell-shaped curve as we saw before, and the area under that curve adds up to 1,000.

HEIGHT

NUMBER OF PEOPLE

Each half of the curve contains 500 heights; half the people in the city are less than average height, and half are taller than average, meaning there's a one in two chance that a person is taller than average and the same chance that they are shorter.

It's easy to find someone who is around average height, but as we move further away from the mean, there are fewer people with these heights.

At each end of the graph, the line almost reaches zero because there are very few people living in the city who are that tall or that short. The tallest and shortest heights are the **outliers**, at the extreme ends of the distribution. There are fewer outlying heights than there are average heights, so the chances of being either the tallest or shortest height are very low.

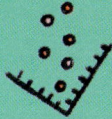

How likely is it?

Statisticians use this system to study more complex sets of data. They look at where one piece of data sits in the bell curve. If the number is near the middle of the curve, then the chances are that it's true. If the data is way out on the edge, then maybe it's not a typical example of what is really happening.

Even so, this way of thinking is based on chance, so there's always the possibility of making a mistake! It's always possible for a system of measurement to go wrong and something that was ignored as being too unlikely could turn out to be exactly true.

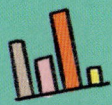

Modern statisticians call these kinds of very unlikely surprises '**black swans**'. The idea for that name comes from a time when everyone living in the Northern Hemisphere thought that all swans were white (adult swans at least). The likelihood of seeing a black swan seemed impossible. However, when a Dutch explorer visited Australia in 1697, what did he find? Black swans! Even though the data said that black swans were so unlikely that we assumed they were not real, they ended up being very real indeed. So statisticians know to think about 'black swans' in data when they are using it to predict what is likely to happen in future.

What happens next?

Data sets are based on measurements of real things. There is always a possibility that they contain mistakes. **Statisticians** use the maths of chance or uncertainty to test their results.

What would happen if there were no measurement mistakes, and every movement and process that made the world work was understood completely? If that was possible, we could figure out exactly what would happen next and keep going on into the future for ever.

However, it is not possible to make exact measurements because there will always be some tiny error somewhere. Even today, we do not understand well enough how atoms and energy work to describe what they will do in the future. It may be that we will never figure this out. Nevertheless, we can use the **maths of chance** to predict what is most likely to happen.

Data scientists also use these techniques to create computer models of complicated processes, such as the way the **world's climate** will change or how a disease spreads through a city. The model is based on many different kinds of data collected from the real world. For example, a climate model contains information about air temperature, air pressure, wind speed, and rainfall, plus a lot more besides.

Scientists from all over the world are figuring out what needs to be measured to make a good model. The American scientist, Kate Marvel, for example, has figured out that the soil, clouds, and the way trees grow are all important for understanding climate change. Marvel tracked changes in soil and tree growth over many years as a way of measuring climate changes that have already happened, to help us understand what might happen in the future.

Once all the data is collected, it is linked together using mathematics—so when one piece of data changes, it influences the others. For example, if clouds increase and block out the sun, the temperature will go down and it might start to rain. However, these links are not fixed. The model introduces **elements of chance** in them—so some of the changes might only be small, sometimes they might be big, but mostly they are about average.

DATA HERO

KATE MARVEL

American climate scientist who collects data about soil, clouds, and the way trees grow, to help make better models that can predict climate change.

Data modelling

This kind of modelling uses numbers to create a copy of something from the real world. Those numbers start out as data collected from the **real world**, but then the model uses the maths of chance to figure out how those values would change as time goes on. This kind of model can come up with predictions or forecasts of what will probably happen far into the future.

Mathematical models like this are very complex and they require the world's biggest computers to run them. The models work very well for forecasting the weather a few days into the future. However, no one can be totally sure that climate models based on data from today and the past can forecast exactly what will happen in many years' time.

One test is to use a model to **hindcast**. That means to run the models backwards, so today's data is used to calculate what was happening yesterday and back into the past.

We're having a downpour in 1868.

A huge storm is on its way!

Then the results produced by the model are checked with what was measured, and the models are then adjusted so they work better.

The same kinds of models are being used to predict what you might do next. Yes, you! How accurate do you think the predictions will be? That depends on what information and data you provide about yourself. How do you feel about your data being used like this? **Let's look at that next.**

Chapter 6

You and Your Data

Now we know a little more about what data is and what it can and can't do, we might wonder what it is recording about us as individuals.

Data always begins with measurements made of a real thing. This can be a population, the Earth, and **it can also be you.** Your **gadgets**—things like a phone, tablet, or computer—are useful devices for accessing all kinds of information, but they are also ways of collecting data *from* you.

Online services like websites, **social media**, video platforms, and games allow you to communicate with other people, play, and learn new things. The companies that make the devices and the apps you use, and provide the services you connect with, are also using these things as data collection tools. This might sound scary at first but let's look into it a bit more and you can decide which bits are good and which might be bad.

Recorded history

One important data set is your personal online history. This is a list of all the web pages you have ever visited, including things like the videos you've watched, the games you've played, and the messages you've sent, and is **unique to you**. Only you did all these things, in this order, at these times.

Historical data from many millions, maybe billions, of people is used by **technology** companies to figure out what people are doing every day, and to predict what they might want to do next.

For example, if you searched the internet with a question:

> ### 'What is the best book ever written?'

the search service will start to look for websites that contain those words. There will be millions of them, and many of those will have nothing to do with your question. The **search engine** uses other data to find a better list of answers. It has data on how often each of these pages gets visited, and it can also cross-check how many of those visits were from people who were searching for the same thing as you. This results in a shorter list of web pages, and one of them will have more visits than the others. This one will probably provide the best answer to the question, and so it appears at the top of the list of search results. All this work is done in a tiny fraction of a second.

Larry Page and Sergey Brin, the two people who set up Google in the 1990s, were experts in data. They created a search **algorithm** that was able to compare all the different kinds of data linked to each web page and then give each one a score based on what was being searched for. This system organized web pages by how useful they were, not just by what words they included.

We invented Google.

You're welcome!

To keep working, this kind of search service needs a fresh supply of your data (and everyone else's). In return for **your data**, the online services are given away for free.

✳ Speak like a scientist ✳

ALGORITHM

An algorithm is a set of instructions arranged in a specific order to solve a problem. Computer programs are made of algorithms.

Google and other web companies make their money by showing you targeted adverts as you surf the web. They use your online data history to show you adverts that you might be interested in. So after searching for 'good books', you might start to see adverts for new books being released. As the search engine collects more data about what you are interested in, it becomes better at choosing adverts that catch your eye.

Making suggestions

A similar system helps people find something new to watch on TV. A video-streaming platform collects plenty of data about its customers. It knows what they like to search for and what they have watched in the past. It also knows its users' age, location, and family members (and what *they* watch). This all helps when we search for something new to watch because the platform will show us things that it believes we will like. This process is called **personalization**.

By comparing the viewing habits of its customers, the system can also identify people who watch similar things and share the same tastes. The system can then recommend items to a viewer based on what it knows they are likely to want to watch, because other people similar to them have enjoyed it.

Search engine data can be **distorted** by one computer sending out the same search request over and over again automatically. The search engine algorithm then thinks this fake search request is more important than it really should be, and that changes what everyone see in their searches. The people that run search engines are always on the look out for these data attacks.

Social data

On social media platforms, we're encouraged to create links with other people and this data is collected. This might be a celebrity that we like to follow, or a channel that makes entertaining posts. We also link with friends and share posts with them.

✳ Speak like a scientist ✳

SOCIAL MEDIA

Social media is the collective name given to online services where the users create the content. We share what we've done, photos we've taken, and videos we've made, with our friends and the world.

Your activity on social media is stored in the same way it is with any other online service. The data is used by algorithms to suggest more videos and memes you might like, and who to follow. It can also make suggestions to find other people that you might know who use the same service. The algorithm is using our data to keep our attention for as long as possible, ensuring that we keep on using its service.

Although people mostly post on social media using a private device, in the comfort of their own homes, their posts are mostly very public. The boundary between what is **public and private** is not so clear on social media. We might say something to a friend in the privacy of our own home that we wouldn't say to a big group of people for example, but sometimes when we use social media it can be easy to forget the difference.

Filter bubbles

Once the algorithm identifies that you like a certain kind of content, it will suggest more and more material that is a close match to it. It won't take a big chance and suggest you watch something completely different because it doesn't want to risk you switching off. The result is called a 'filter bubble', where new ideas—especially those that don't fit with your data profile—are filtered out. This can make it harder for people to learn about different points of view or see the world from another perspective.

Taking control

Social media has probably been around for as long as you can remember. However, it is still a relatively new technology and a new form of communication and entertainment.

Social media works by collecting data from its users. Governments around the world are still trying to figure out how to protect the privacy of these users, while the social media companies need private data to keep working. **Billions** of people also enjoy using those services which are improved by data sharing. Governments can see that the data collected by social media and other platforms can be useful to them too. For example, it could be used to research health and social problems; or private data might be used to track down criminals. In some countries though, private data has been used to find people who don't agree with the leaders in power, and put them in prison!

Once private data has been collected, who decides what happens to it next? Some countries have laws giving users a say over what they want their data to be used for. There, anyone who has private information about you must not share it with a third party, and companies have been fined because they have shared private data. However, our society is still learning how to handle private data in the best way. How and when we share our private data is something for us all to think about.

Using data badly

It's tempting to think that by collecting enough data we can build a better system of communication that will automatically be a good thing for everyone. However, researchers are discovering that we've been making a lot of mistakes and many of the ways our cities, buildings, and cars have been constructed are based on **faulty data.**

Most notably, data was collected about men only and it was simply assumed that systems, like healthcare and public transport, would work for women too. Researchers like Caroline Criado Perez have shown that this is not the case, and that women have been excluded from vast amounts of data.

One good example is air-conditioning systems used in large skyscrapers, designed to remove warm air from the building so it's cool inside. Designers came up with a figure for how much heat the people in the building were giving out but they only used data about how much heat a man's body gives out. A woman's body gives out less heat. That meant that the system removed too much heat, leaving many women in the building feeling cold.

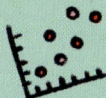

DATA HERO

CAROLINE CRIADO PEREZ

Author and journalist who showed how using biased data to design systems and build machines has meant that women have often been disadvantaged.

Making decisions

Mistakes with data like those highlighted by Caroline Criado Perez affect many other sections of society. Data scientists can learn from these mistakes in the future. This is increasingly important as the information collected about us is being used to make more and more important decisions about our lives. For example, our data is used to figure out whether we can borrow money to buy a house or whether a medical test shows we are ill or healthy. Will these systems make new mistakes? And if they do, how will we know? Let's find out more about how they work.

Chapter 7

Data and the Future

The amount of data in the world is astounding. It is estimated that every day another 1.2 trillion megabytes (MB) is added to the internet.

A photo contains about 1 MB, so 1.2 **trillion** MB is a lot of pictures, as well as emails, videos, and social media posts. It all gets stored in vast data warehouses filled with many thousands of computers. The total amount of data stored in these warehouses is thought to be about 44 zettabytes, which is 44,000 trillion **megabytes** or

44,000,000,000,000,000 MB!

✳ Speak like a scientist ✳

MEGABYTE

This is a measure of how much information is stored in a computer file. One megabyte is a million bytes, and one byte contains eight bits. One numeral, such as a 1 or 0, is a single bit of data. (A gigabyte, or GB, is a thousand megabytes, and a terabyte, or TB, is a million megabytes.)

You might be surprised to know that data has a carbon footprint. Because data is stored on computers, it is estimated that the internet makes up two per cent of the world's carbon emissions, or about a billion tonnes of greenhouse gases, a year.

Changing links

The internet was switched on in 1969. It was originally designed to connect computers together so they could share data easily. The clever part is that the data organizes its own route. If the route is blocked because a connection has broken somewhere, the data just tries another one, ensuring that the messages always get through.

By the year 2000, the internet had transformed into a service that connected people—and soon social media platforms had become the main online services. Today 4.6 billion—more than half of all the people on Earth—use the internet every day.

A lot of the data travelling through the wires is **all about us!**

Now the internet is changing again, into something called the internet of things, meaning any machine with an internet connection. That could be a satellite in space, a weather buoy floating far out in the ocean, some watches, or TVs streaming videos. All of these items are sending and receiving data through the internet. It's predicted that by 2030 there will be 50 billion things sending data into the internet.

Big Data

What are we going to do with all that information? The answer might be Big Data, which is more of an idea than a real thing. The idea comes from the fact that we have so much data coming from so many different sources—and there is more coming all the time. It includes everything from a text message from the pizza delivery service to information about earth tremors under the seabed. However, maybe all this combined data will tell us something? All we have to do is think of new ways to search through it.

The use of Big Data is only just beginning, but the information in there could lead to some very exciting discoveries about new kinds of medicines, figuring out how to deliver parcels across a city as quickly as possible, or ways to help stop climate change. What question would you ask Big Data?

What is the meaning of life?

What will be humans' greatest ever invention?

Will humans ever go to Mars?

Will robots take over one day?

Hidden patterns

One way to understand Big Data is to look for **patterns** between unconnected data sets. There will be many that appear just by coincidence, but some might be very useful to know. For example, the data recording money moving between bank accounts might contain patterns that show when criminals are stealing money. Similarly, information collected about how cars are being driven in the real world, might give car factories information that they can use to build safer and more efficient vehicles in the future.

Clever computers

Human data experts can search for patterns in Big Data. However, the real Big Data expert might be an **artificial** intelligence, or **AI**. An AI is a highly complex algorithm designed to make decisions, so we don't have to. It is able to take in messy, raw data and figure out which bits to ignore and which bits to use to come up with an answer. Some AIs teach themselves how to do this using a system called **machine learning**. The AI gets a lot of help from human programmers, but it learns its job by repeating one task over and over again, millions of times, until it gets it right every time.

The jobs that AIs excel at are the ones that humans find more challenging. For example, AIs power smart speakers. Unlike humans, they are able to listen for commands every minute of every day without getting tired, bored, or annoyed. Other AIs can search medical scans for signs of disease or check the soundtracks of videos to make sure they are not using someone else's music. AIs can do this kind of work faster and better than any human, but they can only do the specific job they were taught to do. Unlike you, an AI does not understand what it does or doesn't know already, and it can't figure out what else it might need to learn to get **smarter**.

Nevertheless, AIs are being developed to do jobs that humans can't do. Sharvari Gujja runs an artificial intelligence laboratory in Boston, USA.

She is creating AIs to investigate how diseases attack the human body by collecting a large amount of data about the chemical processes going on in the body and looking for patterns that might explain why it's getting sick. This kind of data science is called **bioinformatics**. The hope is that the AI will eventually be able to spot very early signs of illness, which can be treated swiftly.

Speak like a scientist

BIOINFORMATICS

Bioinformatics is the science of collecting and analysing data from any living thing. This data can be analyzed to find previously unknown connections, revealing how the human body works and how it changes during illness.

DATA HERO

SHARVARI GUJJA

An American data scientist working with AI technology. Gujja uses data from AIs to better understand the causes of human diseases.

Machine bias

The hope is that AIs can make better decisions than humans because they don't show bias and rarely make mistakes. However, as data experts like Cathy O'Neil have found, if AIs are not set up correctly in the first place, it is possible for them to reflect the biases of the people who create them. **Worse still**, the AI then learns from those biased decisions and so keeps on making the same mistake over and over. For example, some money-lending algorithms use data about where someone lives in order to predict whether they will be able to pay back the loan. If a person lives in a poor neighbourhood, the algorithm predicts they're less likely to pay back the money.

However, the loan might help someone to further their **education**, allowing them to find a well-paid job and pay back the loan.

If a person living in a poor neighborhood isn't able to find a well-paid job and runs into financial difficulty, this is recorded too. When the algorithm checks the area, it sees that people living there often have financial problems and decides they should not get loans, and the problem with the algorithm goes round and round.

DATA HERO

CATHY O'NEIL

American mathematician and author. She has shown that AIs can make biased decisions, making things worse, not better.

What are the results?

Whatever the future holds, data is going to play a very **big part** in both our public and our private lives.

Data gives us the tools to **unlock knowledge** and we're creating new ways of doing that all the time. But there are important questions about how far we are willing to go in this quest: about how we collect private data and what we are using it for, how our own biases and errors can creep into the data and change the meaning we take from it, and the environmental impact that storing all this data has on our world.

Now you know more about data, you can see all the ways it's helping us and what some of the pitfalls may be. The world today is facing some big issues, such as climate change, and there's no doubt that data can be used to explain the world to us and help us find **ways to make it better.**

Data can answer all your questions! What do you want to know?

Glossary

abacus a highly efficient mechanical calculator made from counters or beads strung on rods

AI short for artificial intelligence; a smart computer program that allows machines to make decisions, solve problems, and do jobs that normally need a person

algorithm a set of instructions arranged in a specific order to solve a problem. Computer programs are made of algorithms

artificial made by people, but copying something that is natural

axes the bottom (horizontal) line and the side (vertical) line on a graph, marked at regular intervals with numbers to indicate time, quantity, etc.

biased giving an inaccurate impression, e.g. suggesting something is more important or common than it really is

Big Data the huge amount of information collected from the many billions of gadgets connected to the internet

bioinformatics the science of collecting data from living things and looking for patterns in that data, e.g. to find out how the body works and what happens when it goes wrong

coordinates a set of numbers that describe a point on a graph or in space

correlation when two sets of data *appear* to match, so as one changes, so does the other (though the two may not in fact be linked)

data pieces of information (one piece of information is known as a datum)

data point a point on a graph that represents a fact

distribution the pattern made when all the data points (facts or pieces of data) are plotted onto a graph

engineers people who design, build, and fix machinery

gadgets any small and useful device. A smartphone is a gadget

machine learning a way for a computer to program itself and write its own algorithm, and so become a kind of AI

mean an average calculated by adding together all the numbers in a data set (e.g. how many goals scored by a team) then dividing by the number of values in the same data set (e.g. how many matches the team played)

median an average found by arranging the data set in order from lowest to highest; the median is the number in the middle

megabyte a million bytes of data, where 1 byte = 8 bits (a bit, short for 'binary digit', is the smallest unit of data in computing and is either 0 or 1); so a megabyte is made up of 8 million digits

mode the most common number (the number that appears most often) in a data set

negative when a number is less than zero

numerals the shaped symbols that represent particular numbers

outliers unusual or rare examples of something

personalization when data is used to meet a person's particular needs e.g. to suggest a product a customer might want to buy, based on their internet browsing history

positional numbers a number system based on units, tens, hundreds and so on, always listed in the same order, so 104 always means one hundred, no tens and four units

positive when a number is more than zero

precision how exact a number is

prehistoric from a time before people recorded events in ways that were passed down to later generations as history

probability the chances of something happening or not

psychometric based on how a particular person experiences or feels about something

qualitative descriptive, and based on the nature of something (e.g. a personal experience or an opinion); qualitative data is usually in words rather than numbers

range the difference between the highest and lowest values in a set of data

search engine a service that uses data to find a website that matches what the searcher is asking for

social media online services where the users create the content by posting photos, film clips and text

statistic a result created from data and written as a number; its accuracy is affected by how it is created and what data it is based on

tallies simple marks that represent quantities or numbers

technology the use of the latest scientific knowledge to create new inventions

trillion a million million

visual data data presented in a picture, e.g. a pie chart, bar chart, or line graph, or on a map

Index